PowerKids Readers:

Bilingual Edition

My Library of Holidays™
Edición Bilingüe

Gillian Houghton
Traducción al español:
Tomás González

The Rosen Publishing Group's
PowerKids Press™ & **Editorial Buenas Letras**™
New York

1

Published in 2004 by The Rosen Publishing Group, Inc.
29 East 21st Street, New York, NY 10010

First Edition

Book Design: Michael J. Caroleo

Photo Credits: Cover and pp. 5, 22 (wreath) © Ted Horowitz/CORBIS; pp. 7, 9, 12, 22 (stockings) © CORBIS; pp. 11, 15, 17, 19, 21, 22 (presents, Santa Claus, and ornaments) © Digital Vision; p. 22 (candycanes) by Cindy Reiman.

Houghton, Gillian
     Christmas = Navidad / Gillian Houghton ; translated by Tomás González.
          p. cm. — (My library of holidays)
     Includes bibliographical references and index.
     Summary: This book introduces the celebration of Christmas, the holiday that honors Jesus' birth, and describes the traditions of decorating Christmas trees, sending Christmas cards, giving gifts, and singing carols.
     ISBN 1-4042-7524-X (lib.)
     1. Christmas—Juvenile literature   [1. Christmas   2. Holidays
3. Spanish language materials—Bilingual]   I. Title   II. Series
     GT4985.5.H6813 2004   2003-010264
     394.2663—dc21

Manufactured in the United States of America

Contents

Contenido

When winter begins and Christmas is near, we place a wreath on our front door.

Cuando empieza el invierno y se acerca la Navidad, colocamos una guirnalda en la puerta de nuestra casa.

5

Christmas is a Christian holiday. Christians are people who follow the teachings of Jesus. They honor Jesus' birth on Christmas day, December 25.

La Navidad es una fiesta cristiana. Los cristianos son personas que siguen las enseñanzas de Jesús. Honran el nacimiento de Jesús el 25 de diciembre, el día de la Navidad.

My family gathers to enjoy the holiday together.

Mi familia se reúne para celebrar la Navidad.

We put ornaments and candy canes on a tree. We put a star on the top of the tree.

Ponemos adornos y dulces en forma de bastón en el árbol de Navidad. Colocamos una estrella en la parte más alta del árbol.

We hope that our stockings will be filled with gifts on Christmas morning.

Esperamos que nuestros calcetines estén llenos de regalos en la mañana de la Navidad.

13

We ask Santa Claus for gifts and for good luck.

Le pedimos a Santa Claus que nos traiga regalos y buena suerte.

We send cards to family and friends. We write about our hopes for the coming year. We wish our friends a happy Christmas.

Enviamos tarjetas a nuestros familiares y amigos.
Les contamos nuestros deseos para el año que viene. Les deseamos una feliz Navidad.

We walk from house to house singing carols. A carol is a joyful song about Christmas.

Caminamos de casa en casa cantando villancicos. Los villancicos son canciones alegres que celebran la Navidad.

19

We give presents to the people we love. Christmas is a time for being kind.

En Navidad damos regalos a nuestros seres queridos.
La Navidad es una época para compartir.

Words to Know
Palabras que debes saber

candy canes
dulces

ornaments
adornos

presents
regalos

Santa Claus

stockings
calcetines

wreath
guirnalda

Here are more books to read about Christmas /
Otros libros que puedes leer sobre la Navidad:

In English/En inglés:
A Christmas Star
by Linda Oatman High
Holiday House

The Polar Express
by Chris Van Allsburg
Houghton Mifflin

Too Many Tamales
by Gary Soto
Putnam

In Spanish/En español:
Navidad en familia
de Kestutis Kasparavicius
Fondo de Cultura Económica

Due to the changing nature of Internet links,
PowerKids Press has developed an online list of
Web sites related to the subject of this book.
This site is updated regularly. Please use this
link to access the list:

http://www.buenasletraslinks.com/hol/nav

Index

Índice

Words in English: 142   Palabras en español: 157

Note to Parents, Teachers, and Librarians
PowerKids Readers books *en español* are specially designed for emergent Hispanic readers and students learning Spanish in the United States. Simple stories and concepts are paired with photographs of real kids in real-life situations. Sentences are short and simple, employing a basic vocabulary of sight words, as well as new words that describe familiar things and places. With their engaging stories and vivid photo-illustrations, PowerKids *en español* gives children the opportunity to develop a love of reading and learning that they will carry with them throughout their lives.